UNDERSTANDING HER

"For Her, From Him"

Authors:

ANA RITA COMPIO REYES

BIMBY MACBS

ISBN:
Hardbound-978-621-470-461-3
MOBI/KINDLE-978-621-470-462-0
Softbound/Paperback-978-621-470-463-7

Published by:
Poetry Planet Book Publishing House
Rosario, Pozorrubio, Pangasinan, Philippines
Contact Number: 09554960094
Email: maritesritumalta@gmail.com

Dedication

This book is dedicated to all husbands, and men (adult and young adult) to love every woman not because they are your wife, your mother, your sister, or friend but because they are human and they are your co-maker in building a beautiful and transforming world to live in.

A Real Man
never hurts a woman.
Be very careful when
you make a woman cry.
Because God counts
her tears. The woman
came out of man's rib.
Not from his feet to be
walked on. Not from
his head to be superior.
But from his side to be
equal. Under the arm
to be protected.
And next to the heart
to be loved.

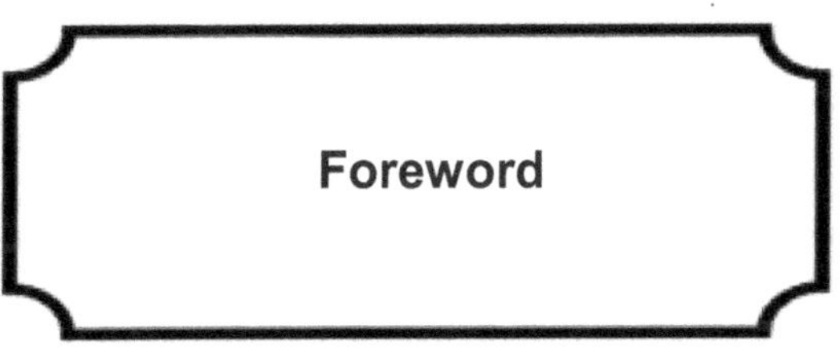

Foreword

It takes 21 days to form a habit and 90 days to make it a permanent habit

This is a gentleman's guide that provides details on how to have emancipating power over your relationship.

Everyone aims for a rewarding and fulfilling relationship that does not dwell on physical intimacy but more on emotional and intellectual connection.

Having a real gentlemanly habit will help transform your current relationship or your future affair into a celebration of bliss and soulful commitment. You will appreciate the gesture of participating rather than anticipating several issues that may dwell in your bond as a lover.

This is a self-help book that acts as food for every young, single, in-relationship man and even married man who always overlooked the importance of a sustainable and procreating love affair that should be vested in nurturing character.

We always thought that once we get the "Yes" of our lady we can gradually stop our sensitivity and our zest.

Women hate men who sleep in the middle of their phone conversations. Women don't like to receive snide remarks or jokes coming from you when they are with their peers. Women pretend to be okay when you are late for your appointment and will act nonchalantly. Most women are meticulous in their appearance each time they go on date or even in casual shopping so, never take this matter for granted.

These inappropriate behaviors of a man should be lessened and must be extinguished from his system.

This book will provide you with 21 habits that will facilitate helping you achieve an attainable and smart relationship.

Character rediscovery should be learned by heart, establish by the mind and perform by hands while building an empire of love for the woman you certainly cherish.

It is not just about love that will bring wellness to your affair but it is also about your habit that will spell good influence in the tale that you hope to live to tell.

TABLE OF CONTENTS

Dedication 3

Foreword.. 5

Habit 1 " Sunny Side Up" 11

Habit 2 " Bake It On Time" 15

Habit 3 “Butter Up” 19

Habit 4 " Chew it over " 23

Habit 5 "No Room For Huge_Mushroom"..27

Habit 6 "Pizza Prayer"............................... 32

Habit 7 " With Bells On" 37

Habit 8 "Bacon Express" 41

Habit 10 " Dirty Spaghetti"......................... 46

Habit 11 "Emptying the cup”...................... 50

Habit 12 ¨ Drink A Tea Of Responsibility¨ .54

Habit 13¨No Cheat Meal On_A Cheat Day 57

Habit 14 ¨ Surprise, French Fries! ¨ 61

Habit 15 ¨ Cloudy MeatBalls ¨................... 65

Habit 16 " Angry Hamburger" 68

Habit 17 " Be My Ribs, Spareribs"............ 72

Habit 18 " Food Give And Forgive............ 75

Habit 19 "Scream, Ice Cream" 78

Habit 20 "Marinara Sauce ... 81 vs. Fettucini Sauce" 81

Habit 21 " Overjoy ChickenJoy"................85

Final Habit "Epilogue" 89

ABOUT THE AUTHORS 90

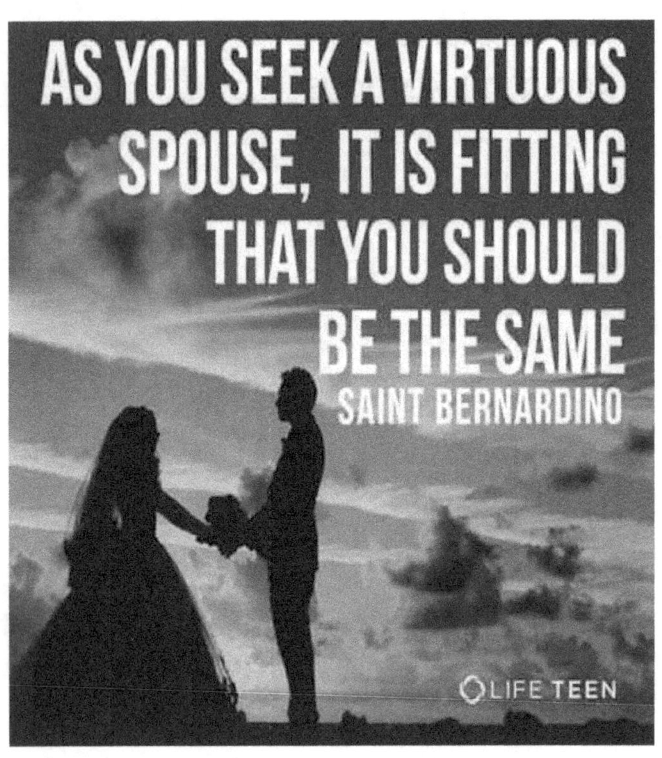
AS YOU SEEK A VIRTUOUS
SPOUSE, IT IS FITTING
THAT YOU SHOULD
BE THE SAME
SAINT BERNARDINO
LIFE TEEN

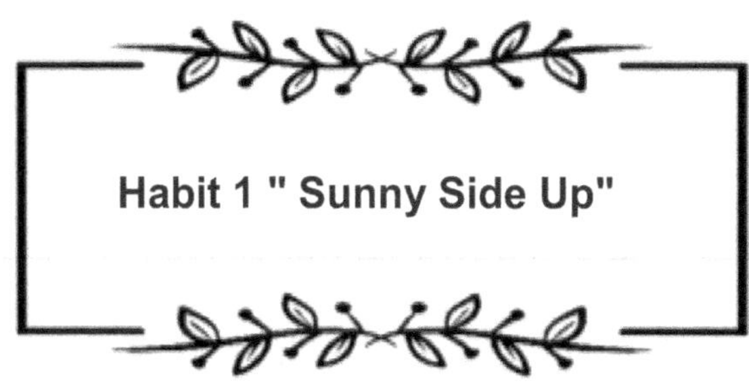

Habit 1 " Sunny Side Up"

Men were raised to be independent and should have a strong sense of autonomy.

In a relationship, it is quite okay to be clingy sometimes but always remember that you are two separate individuals united only by a common bond which is love. Aside from love, your personal identity is not attached to that relationship. That is a common mistake of every couple because they often put their personal concern on the shoulder of their partner.

Your partner is not a superhero. She is not a sponge to absorb everything. She is not a washing machine to wash away your blues and spin dry you. Unless she asks you thrice then that is the time you will profess gently the concerns that bother you.

Issues about finances or your own debts are not your girlfriend's or fiancée's burden to keep. Help yourself in such a situation by looking for a decent means to get away from that trouble.

Sometimes it is down-grading to see a man who is dependent on a woman. Nowadays women became the bread and butter of some men. I see a woman working 8-10 hours a day while her boyfriend is waiting outside their office to fetch her and after which they will have a cozy dinner paid by the woman and to make the night more romantic this woman will give a gift to his boyfriend which is a pair of popular shoes. She is 24 years old to be a sugar mommy! She can't even spend 500 bucks to visit her dentist to extract her decaying canine tooth but she will spend all her salary on her parasitic boyfriend.

It is a poor statement to hear that "I will not look for a girlfriend because it is expensive ". Where did you get that idea? Most of the women are praiseworthy of even small details. They understood that a relationship is not about spending and dining to make it colorful. Women are happy to see their man giving them letters and roses from a neighbor's garden. This simple act of love is not yet outmoded and it speaks louder than your monotony of saying “I love you”.

You can run into a garden barefoot with your girlfriend and chase some butterflies or dragonflies as one of your thrilling moments together. Your woman will appreciate it dearly.

If you really want a grandeur date, find a job. There are several works out there. But please, do not borrow money from a friend or from your mom just for a date. That is totally a huge injury to your backbone.

The adversary of independence is shame and doubt. So if you don't want to swim in a pond of shame and climb the ladder of doubt, be a man, build a productive attitude wherein you are investing in temporal necessities and emotional soundness.

Marriage is an adventure, like going to war.
- G.K. Chesterton -
The Catholic Gentleman

Habit 2 " Bake It On Time"

Time is of essence.

Punctuality is a skill that every man should master. They say that "Better late than sorry" but you will feel sorry if that will be the cause of your major fight.

Being right on time is an attitude that depicts that you are dependable. Your partner or girlfriend will think that you are reliable and you can be trusted. If you are careless with time, she will have an intuition that "If you are careless with time, how much more in many things like our relationship".

Time is always of the essence. If you are already in a relationship you should know the value of time that you give and take from your partner.

You have an appointment at 8:00 am and you arrive at 9:00 am. You know how much time you wasted and how disrespectful you are with her time. If you can't come at an exact hour do not make a commitment and an appointment. Women will accept several excuses but they can't understand why you need to run with a realistic alibi (such as traffic, wrestling with a drunk man, or being gore by a carabao) if you can avoid it.

Michael Learns to Rock song “25 minutes" He was 25 minutes too late. If he just arrives on time then he must have the best thing in life. This implies that he took the girl for granted and he has no certainty.

You are not in school and everything is a practice, plus trial and error. This is a real relationship and you are obliged to be a man of the time.

Time is gold and life is a race. How many millions will go stale if a certain multi-corporation can't deliver its products to its end-user at the right time?

How many lives will be diminished if the doctor fails to give medication right on time to an emergency patient?

Always remember that waiting has its limit but punctuality has its own reward.

We often hear the words "Quality time and "Quantity Time" but we forget the most important component of these two which is the value of time which is tantamount to punctuality.

It can only be quality time if you start it at the right time and it becomes quantity time if the allotted time was utilized well.

Love will flourish at the exact time and right place so do not delay it by using these schemes of this time frame:

Shower = 24 minutes
6 minutes = wash and rinse body
20 minutes = reflection and deep thoughts about the origin of life and the universe.
1 hour= of sleeping in the tub

How do you enjoy your two-hour bath?

One man's "I don't know" is another man's
"I knew from the moment I saw her."
-unknown

Habit 3 “Butter Up”

If your girlfriend, fiancée, or wife tells you that "I miss you", it does not follow that she misses you physically. She might be saying about the old you or the usual routine that you have done to her while you are still courting.

Not giving attention to the things she missed about you is an insensitive failure of affection. A real gentleman is sensitive enough in comprehending the emotion behind every word of his lover.

There are some verbal responses that a man should be keen on deciphering. The word “I miss you" could mean that she is missing you because she can't have your full attention. There are instances that you are with her, and everything that you talk about is how jerk is your boss in dumping you into another department. Or instead of sitting beside you and pampering you with a massage on your head, you were too apathetic and you keep playing Mobile Legends while letting her wonder if she is still part of your plan.

When a girl says "I miss you" from out of nowhere while both of you are doing your weekly grocery, she just wants you to grab her favorite shampoo and appreciate her beautiful hair. She wants you to remember the usual stuff that you both love cooking every weekend to rekindle memories.

Guys often miss several opportunities to be romantic and empathetic. They dwell on what can satisfy them without giving gratification to the woman they love. They believe that simply saying "I love you" and a kiss will satisfy the loneliness of the heart of their partner but they don't understand that woman needs more reinforcement to feel that they are truly loved and they are special.

Every woman is their father's first love and when they say "I miss you" they long for the love that their father had given to them. She expected that the love you will give is sincere and pure. She wanted to be treated like a princess and heiress. She wanted that you as a partner will share in her longingness for his father. It is not using you as an outlet but as an image of what she wants in a man.

"What can I say, I like to see people run to each other, I like the kissing and the crying, I like the impatience, the stories that the mouth can't tell fast enough, the ears that aren't big enough, the eyes that can't take in all of the change, I like the hugging, the bringing together, the end of missing someone" -Jonathan Safran Foer.

Marriage is to help married people **sanctify *themselves and others***. For this reason **they receive a special grace in the sacrament** which Jesus Christ instituted. *Those who are called to the married state will, with the grace of God, find within their state* ***everything they need to be holy.***

(Saint Josemaria Escriva)

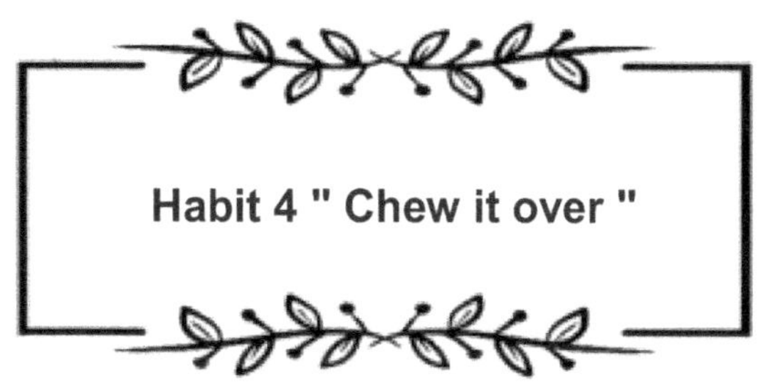

Habit 4 " Chew it over "

To begin with a sweet and exciting conversation with your future girlfriend, fiancée, or wife, start it with simple compliments. Ask her why she wears that beautiful smile and how her makeup complements the radiance of her skin. Remind her that her last hairstyle was as glamorous as she has right now. Compliment her choices in food, restaurant, books, and jewelry. A simple appreciation of her will make her feel that she is your world.

Women are fun of expressing their feelings in a vague and ambiguous statement which is why a man should sharply observe it. If your lady tells you that “I love your biceps" she wanted to hear from you that her figure is amazing and how did she maintain such a beautiful body physique. If she said “I like it when you hug me" she just wanted to hear how much your presence is of importance. She wanted to feel and hear that the way she cares for you is the best expression of love.

Every woman takes extra effort to make their appearance appealing and exciting in your presence and all they need is your validation to make them feel satisfied through your sweet words of encouragement. The best ego-booster is simple and genuine words of appreciation coming from someone you love. It adds glory to your days and it can fulfill your emotional soundness too.

However, be careful of complimenting your partner because it could be redundant and inappropriate. There are instances when you wanted to make her happy and you say complimentary words at the wrong time and at the wrong place which will put her in complete embarrassment.

Learn more history about your partner and have thorough knowledge about areas of her body that she always avoid discussing. For instance, you brought her a pair of pearl earrings and told her that "This pair of pearl earrings will make you look like a star of the sea or will make you as beautiful as Ariel. This will add as well radiance to your soft ears." That is both an overstatement and an understatement. A woman doesn't like to be compared with anyone even with mythical creatures like a mermaid and the worst side is, you are insulting your girlfriend by telling her that the pearl earrings will add radiance to her ears. What if your girlfriend has ears larger than Roger Rabbit? How could you be so apathetic to say those words? Your gesture of cheerfulness is jeopardized by your being tactless.

Do not exaggerate things. Make sure that when you are praising your partner it is simple, clear, and directly coming from the heart so that her heart can accept it with gusto and enthusiasm.

Another tip is to avoid the usage of slang words in providing praises to your girlfriend. You are not Snoopy Dog to say "Drop it like it's hot " to your better half. This is totally and beyond doubt an act of disrespect. Be on guard with your words. You could say the word “beautiful” instead of “sexy” or “pretty” instead of “smoking hot”. Your girlfriend doesn't have dengue fever to be called hot. Always remember the usage of appropriate words depicts how you were raised by your parents.

If a marriage is to
preserve its initial charm
and beauty, both husband
and wife should try to
renew their love day after
day, and that is done
through sacrifice, with
smiles and also with
ingenuity.
St. Josemaria Escrivá

Habit 5 "No Room For Huge Mushroom"

"You're smart and cute but you don't need to brag about it on this dinner table".

A little sugar couldn't hurt you but too much of it can be a danger to your blood.

Women see high regard for men who are confident and have a strong sense of pride. Being assertive and self-reliant is equated with self-worth thus, it matters among women because they want their man to be someone with nobility and who can face anyone at a given time and place.

However, the worst-case scenario is often encountered by women on their first date. Some men would always offer a variety of topics to tickle the heart of the woman she is dating and one of which is bragging about the nature of his lifestyle, business, and achievement.

You are not in an interview to sell yourself. This is not a crucial conference to close a business deal and you need to divulge all your aces.

You are facing a woman who will be your future partner in life. A woman who will love you in poverty or in luxury.

You don't need to mention that you have five funeral parks on the whole island to excite the desire of the girl you are dating. It is prohibited to inform and narrate to the woman you are dating that after your grandfather will succumb, you will inherit the 50 hectares of seedless soursop and sugar apple orchard in Area 51.

Who cares about it? Only a few women are materialistic in nature. Most women desire a man who is just confident in what he says and duly acts on what he promised.

Stop mentioning names of high-profile friends to increase your value. The real value of a man can be found in his meekness and humility even though he has the capacity to bluster.

Another point that you need to remember is to stop including a topic about the number of girls you've dated. Do not expect a kiss from a first-time date just because you told her that your previous date was more sensual and intimate. You are facing a different woman. If you dated a girl before with a janitor fish characteristic do not conclude that your recent date will be the same.

If your tongue is too careless to speak about your previous dates and relationship, better fill your whole buccal mucosa with a mouth-watering tuna sandwich to stop it from saying inadequate words. A woman likes a man with an efficient character than a mouth full of volume.

It is improper and unbecoming of a gentleman to speak of your past experiences to someone you just meet for the sake of self-gratification. She would think and realize that you are not a secret keeper and she will conclude that you are a kiss and tell the guy.

It takes a smart man to connect with the mind of a woman but it takes a humble man to open her heart.

Leave your ego and your pride inside your pocket and spontaneously talk and act with politeness and humility to the one you are dating.

A relationship where you
can pray, worship and
passionately pursue God
together, is always worth
the wait.

Habit 6 "Pizza Prayer"

There is a big difference when you are both in the church from you are both in Christ.

Men in the Bible history are usually instructed by God to be a strong shelter and powerhouse of prayer. The spring and fountain of hope and graces will steadfastly flow if a man centered God in his life. He will bring good fortune to his family and his generation if he constantly follows the Divine Will.

A relationship should always be under the state of grace. If you are the reason why your woman becomes adverse to God then you are accountable for that.

Purity and chastity will never be outmoded. It is very imperative in a relationship that you stay away from any stimuli or situation that will lead you to sin.

90 percent of Losing and gaining grace happened before marriage, so you don't go on date without the purpose of getting married. When a relationship started with sin such as fornication (premarital sex) the repercussion of sin will affect the future of married unless it was repented to God.

The worst part of being a woman is being fantasized about by a man. Man must ignore those lustful thoughts and strive to develop a wholesome discipline as a couple.

It is wise and best to wear a wedding dress before buying a baby dress.

Encourage your girlfriend or your wife to set a daily appointment with God through prayer. This will give you a better view of the true meaning of love because you have a constant connection with our Maker who will guide and lead you to the path of righteousness.

It is coined in the scripture that "Two or three gathered in His name, He will be in the midst of us". How will God feel when He sees two of His creations whom He designed to be together, come in His presence to worship Him?

No man is good enough to handle a relationship without seeking the advice of his God.

There are several troubling relationships and broken marriages because the pro-creator of the relationship which is the man has a weak spiritual affinity.

Always remember that a man of strong faith will have a better understanding and patience if troubles come. He will never recourse to a wrong decision but he will have several wise judgments over certain relationship turmoil.

Every woman needs a Godly man who will draw them closer to God.

A loyal and decent woman is a treasure for a man and a faithful and prayerful man is enough for a woman.

It is an amazing blessing for a woman to see her man who has a lip for praising God in the shadow of troubles instead of cursing. It is pleasing to see those strong hands raising and lifting up everything to our Lord God in a moment of desolation instead of beating and hurting his girlfriend or wife.

A true gentleman lover will consume a woman's time but not her weakness, will touch her heart but not her purity, will give her sufficient freedom but will not take away her identity and most of all will pray for her even if they marry already.

THE *greatest mission*
OF TWO PEOPLE IN LOVE
IS TO HELP ONE ANOTHER
BECOME MORE A MAN
AND MORE A WOMAN.
Love IS THUS A KIND
OF *craftsmanship*.
WORD on FIRE

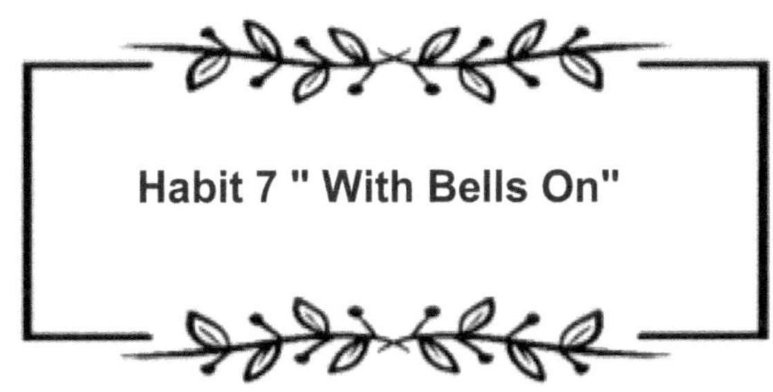

Habit 7 " With Bells On"

Good manner matters, Good look is a bonus but humor is a must.

Having candid behavior and a comical personality enriched a relationship. It builds a strong connection between the two lovers. If there is no fun and excitement in a relationship, the affair becomes stifled and boring.

God has a sense of humor and it can be seen in a man's language and laughter.

The woman doesn't like a stiff and stern man. She wanted to enjoy the company of a man who has so many interesting stories. The woman shows interest in a man who could laugh at his own mistake and who is witty in his words. Most women will agree that humor is tailored to fit the key to their hearts.

Being humorous is an efficient way of building a new relationship. If you know how to speak and act candidly with a woman you must first meet it will diminish the feeling of awkwardness. It is a great aid in starting an open communication because it will allow you to be spontaneous and quick in responding with less embarrassment.

A man with a funny character is the best partner in life. He is optimistic and his outlook in life is enlivened by the spirit of positivity and courage. He can easily deal with several issues that may arise in the relationship and he will always have the option to think and act with determination and hope because of his clear vision of life.

Humor serves as a catch basin and a valuable remedy for stress and frustration. It is also a definite buffer for disappointments and bad patches in a relationship.

The laugh of a man is contagious and his humor can change the mood of his woman. Your girlfriend or wife will find it sweet and thoughtful if you display your childlike playfulness. It will loosen her hostility towards you in times of disagreement.

Good humor is an expression of a man's wisdom. In an argument, a man who can expressively utter his thinking creatively will have the best say in everything.

Humor that is free from sarcasm will help achieve a nurturing relationship. Humor should not cover the truth and it should be clear and pure so that it will not compromise facts and reality. You can't make foolish excuses why you are unreachable for five days because you played the role of Quasimodo (Hunchback of Notre Dame) to earn something to buy your fiancée an engagement ring. Always remember that a clean joke is not deceitful and harmful.

You can't enforce humor but you can develop a sense of joy if you know how to be resilient and be satisfied.

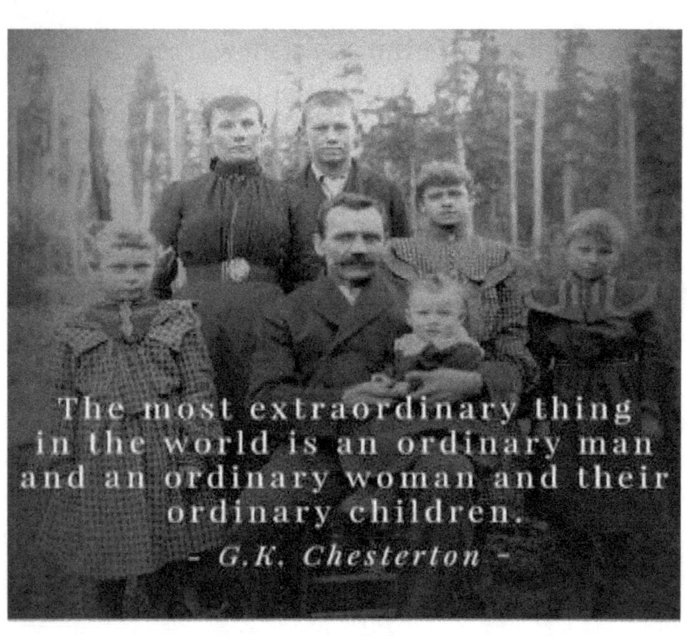
The most extraordinary thing
in the world is an ordinary man
and an ordinary woman and their
ordinary children.
- G.K. Chesterton -

Habit 8 "Bacon Express"

You can be quick but do not be in a hurry. Always remind yourself that haste makes a lot of clutter and waste.

Men often contain themselves in a world where everything should have a specific time frame. Yes, it is a fact that man should know his priority and obligation yet, it does not require him to put pressure and urgent demand on that needs.

Success has no due date as well as love.

Why are you in a hurry? For what prize awaits you?

The vocation to be married must need time, and you have to ask these two questions before you plummet to this idea. Is God my first choice? Am I mature and capable to raise and sustain a family for the long term? Most of the time, if our vocation is wrong and we choose our own will, we will receive only a minimum of grace from God.

Well, I believe that love is blind, love conquers all and I am not stereotyping however, sometimes we choose to open the wrong package due to our quick response. Like the song that says that "It is sad to belong to someone else when the right one comes along".

Relationships and partnerships in marriage or girlfriend/boyfriend love affairs do not require specific dates. It only requires maturity, productive age, and the capacity to be patient and enduring but it is not time-bounded.

There are many young men who are too earnest in finding their dreams and became a failure because their interest is focused on one goal. They become engrossed in forming their dreams but they never had sufficient knowledge to organize their thoughts on how to achieve those dreams.

It goes the same way as finding a girlfriend or a future wife. Some men require beauty, a scholastic profile, and the family background of a woman with whom they will spend their time, talent, and treasure. Because of that, they forgot the essence of love through destiny, fate, and gifts.

We all want to end up with the woman we made in our imagination but the sad reality leads us to a more confusing realm of a love affair. We find love because of our fast and quick choices, because we are afraid of risking and waiting. Sometimes we never based our relationship on our personal affection but on our space and time reference.

We are like the movie “Fast and Furious" and it is a cardinal sign of being greedy, insecure, and impatient. We can see several couples who are not genuinely happy because they force the relationship instead of letting love find a path for them to meet and flourish. Patience is always a virtue and a full-time job of the wise and the idleness of the stupid.

Women are more likely attracted to men who are steady. They find comfort in men who have decisive characteristics but know how to take every step at a time. Women get seriously offended by men who will force them to do something they don't want at the expense of the wrong usage of love and trust. That is why we have a number of women who at an early age get pregnant because of having aggressive, reckless, and irresponsible boyfriends. Everything is fast and instant.

Being a gentleman is determined by your calmness and stillness in a fast pace situation. Being patient is an extraordinary characteristic. Patience can be best described by the saying "Remember to halt before your response".

Part of God's design for the
sanctification of your soul is the
influence which your ***wife*** is
going to have on you.
- FR. RONALD KNOX -

Habit 10 " Dirty Spaghetti"

Good smell and good grooming are important in man's health and proneness.

It is a fact that personal outlook and whole person attributes by a man's exude definitely isn't the salient thing that will entice women to like and love him. However, we must face the harsh reality that a woman will not date a man who looks and smells like the last skunk on earth.

A woman deserves a man who acts and thinks cleanly. A man who knows good grooming is a man with a great deal.

Woman don't want to invest their time going around a guy whose teeth has a hard deposit of tartar which is 5 inches thick like margarine. If there is a best in a gown in a women's beauty pageant, your girlfriend deserves a man who is best in gums too.

You will never have another second date if you act like a beast while dating. Some bad habits like picking the nose, burping like a gorilla, and talking while the mouth is full of mushrooms are inexcusable. These behaviors are rude and you are just making the wrong road for your love life.

It is not your dream to be kept in private by your lover. You don't want to be considered as a hidden or secret boyfriend because your partner is embarrassed to introduce you to her set of friends for the reason that you seldom take a bath, you never change your underwear in a week, and your skin is as dry and as hard as the legs of a cock. This could hurt you but you are the one who is creating your little hell.

Personality-wise attitude does not require certain rituals and items to look tidy. You don't need to wear the top of lines clothing and wear the most expensive perfume to look adorable. Smart casual clothing and a fresh scent are all you need to win the heart of your lady.

A woman needs a pleasing personality in a man and this impeccable look needs to be obvious, from well-cut hair on your head to shoes that are polished and align with the rest of your image.

Good personality and grooming are also punctuated with good disposition and habits.

You must speak with decency and modesty every time and you must be careful with the usage of words. Do not converse using words that may sound piggy and obnoxious.

Being a gentleman is not only calibrated by your values but it can be identified too by how you take care of yourself.

THE CATHOLIC GENTLEMAN
Love which leads to marriage and family, can also be a marvellous divine way, a vocation, a path for a complete dedication to our God.
- ST. JOSEMARIA ESCRIVA -

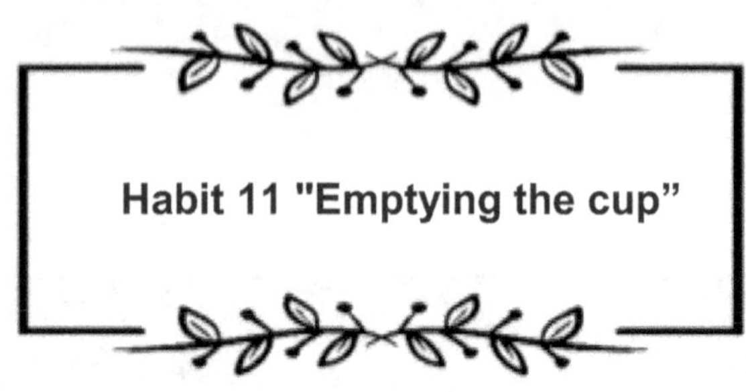

Habit 11 "Emptying the cup”

How do you counterpoise your weakness? How do you motivate yourself? Do you allow your girlfriend or your wife to suffer from your own hurts?

After a sad breakup, you wanted to start a new relationship but the common dilemma is when you are stuck with your own vicious past experiences. That would be unfair and unjust for your partner to partake in your own misery which she is clueless about and has no involvement whatsoever.

We all know that painful events from the distant past can be damaging. Men are considered to have a low and short acceptance for emotional agitation and distress more specifically if this is about relationship breakups.

Men become too weary and doubtful because of the thinking that they might suffer the same fate all over again.

Men who have just undergone an early relationship breakup tend to be very cynical about love. They become less sensitive but more suspicious of the intention of their new partner as they go along with a fresh start in a relationship. They don't want to accept reason because they will always rationalize that they know everything and they survive such concern before therefore, every new relationship will go to early extinction.

Women will have a hard time understanding a man who has a lot of excess baggage. It is a burden for a woman to be in a relationship with a man who is wounded and will never cooperate in his healing. Women are expecting a man who has few dramas and will not be dependent on her emotionally.

The most harrowing and grueling wound is a huge bruise that affects one's soul. It will deeply wound the ego together with the inner part of his emotion. That is why there is no salve for a bruised ego and no cure for an injured emotion. But there is always a remedy.

A man who sustained harm from betrayal and cheating can be pacified by true love.

It is not the role of a woman to be a temporary antidote for a man's pain. Women are not a panacea or a magic bullet that will fix every man's broken heart because they too have an ordeal to face. But they can be an advocate, a motivator, and a giver of love. They can only do that much and it is man's job to help his own rehabilitation.

A man who experiences several defeats in a relationship should know how to empty himself independently. He doesn't need anyone, especially a woman to provide a solution for his emotional weakness. He needs to unload all the anxiety and hatred that he harbored in his heart.

It is not an easy task to unload all your hurts especially when they maim your life but it can be done through willingness and of course the help of God.

The formula for emptying yourself should be gradual but certain and it will begin from whole aches to specific hurts.

The love of husband and wife is the force that welds society together.
- St. John Chrysostom -
The
CATHOLIC GENTLEMAN

Habit 12 ¨ Drink A Tea Of Responsibility¨

Never play a game of blaming your partner over certain issues and concern that arises. Always own your mistake and take responsibility for them.

Imagine a scenario in which a man blames his girlfriend that he was late for work because his girlfriend forgot to wake him up which should be his responsibility. This issue will extend into different clashes of concerns that will eventually lead to a lack of trust and confidence in your partner.

Having emotional intelligence or maturity is a product of responsibility. Exercising accountability is a healthy expression of trust.

Owning a mistake and being accountable is a strength. It encourages you to be honest and demonstrate that you are genuine and authentic. Taking responsibility is an empowering strategy by which you are sincere in your role as a partner and a friend who will never make excuses for your ill-doing but rather choose to face the issue with an open spirit and the purpose of executing a solution.

It is ideal sometimes that you carry too the burden of your partner. A relationship is not just "You and I" but an "Us" which expresses the desire to alleviate your partner's issues, have each other's back, and be driven towards a nurtural relationship. The goal of every relationship is to give a fair level of equity in every responsibility. It can be done by nurturing each other through the process of selfless conveyance of affection, support, and obligation.

Taking responsibility in a relationship does not dwell only on your misbehavior or task that you forgot to fulfill but it is also about managing your emotions and feelings. You may allow your emotion to be recognized by your partner when you are upset or mad but adding hostility and other mixed moods may result in deeper conflict thus you must avoid it. Always be responsible and guard your emotions by distinguishing them from mere emotion or reasoning with knowledge.

THE CATHOLIC GENTLEMAN
The most *extraordinary* thing in the world is an *ordinary* man and an *ordinary* woman and their *ordinary* children.
- G.K. CHESTERTON -

Habit 13¨No Cheat Meal On A Cheat Day

We often hear this saying that ¨ When that cat's away the mice will play¨ hey dude this is not applicable to you.

Being involved in a relationship is a pure and wholesome commitment. It encompasses honesty which is the product of love and security. Just because your girlfriend or wife has a weekend vacation with her friends you are free to do whatever you want such as spending more time in cyberspace and going out with friends with a bunch of chicks.

Commitment in a relationship is a vow that you will continue to remain faithful no matter what the circumstances, set-back, and flaws that you will find out in your journey together. You will never take the opportunity to succumb to temptation if you are given the circumstances that make it possible to do something.

Cheating is a choice and not cheating is a good choice. We may say that in our modern world, most men cheat and it is normal. No, it is not normal and actually, cheating is not a matter of leverage for masculinity or being a stereotype of the male gender. Let us remember that in the context of the Bible, the first person who recognized and accept temptation is Eve and then cascade it to Adam. But let us not be frantic about this because cheating is not attached to any gender, it is a matter of choice and willingness to withstand or yield to it.

Cheating is not only about dating another woman when you are in a relationship or married. Posting pictures of your celebrity crush, or popular woman on social media on your Instagram and putting it on your ¨My Day¨ or Facebook status for the purpose of just being a fan is not acceptable particularly if you shared a commitment with someone.

Watching pornographic films by which you are more sexually aroused by the scene than your intimate moment with your partner is considered as cheating. Cheating is not just about physical contact with someone outside your relationship.

Cheating can be done through the innocent like exchanging text messages ¨Chexting¨ to your female friend or fellow worker specifically if it has nothing rational reason for communication or of importance. Confiding your emotion to a female friend about your issues in concern with your partner where you find an emotional connection with someone than your girlfriend or wife is emotional cheating. If you are deeply in love with your partner your emotional bond will never be tainted by others' sympathy and affection.

The highly destructive and damaging issue in a relationship is the failure to bind to fidelity. It is an uphill battle that only a gentleman with an unconditional sense of emotional and spiritual soundness will have the faculty to overcome it.

Husbands should love their wives as their own bodies. He who loves his wife loves himself.
- St. Paul the Apostle -
The Catholic Gentleman

Habit 14 ¨ Surprise, French Fries! ¨

"The purest and most thoughtful minds are those which love color the most."
— John Ruskin,

Throwing a surprise party because it's your partner's birthday, your anniversary (nowadays Millennial celebrate Daysary, Weeksary, and Monthsary) or she receives a promotion on her job is a common template in a relationship. Although it gives spark and joy to your partner for making her realize how you value and appreciate her yet that is likely to happen and most men do that to their partner and in some cases, it has a little significant value.

How about coming to your wife or girlfriend's office and bringing her flowers and sending her to her favorite restaurant even without an official celebration? In the spur of the moment, you just wanted to celebrate her presence in your life and let her feel how important she is. How will she feel about it? Would it give her a sense of real belongingness and feeling of great importance because you still bestow courtship even if you are exclusively in a relationship or married?

Most women love to be surprised. Women are known to be detailed in everything thus providing more details through unexpected astonishment by surprises will feel rewarding and valued which will be a lifetime memory.

A slight change in the day-to-day routine and incorporating it with love will bring up a sustainable relationship. If your partner used to bring you a cup of coffee every morning, why not cook for her for breakfast? A little twist in routine to fuel your love will have a mile of good repercussions.

Knowing where to tickle the heart of your partner is an essential part of being a gentleman. Chivalry will never die. It is a dormant characteristic in every man that needs to be promoted at a younger age to foster a community of respect and love for every woman.

Always pondering that sweet and good surprises with ingenuity to the woman you love are as gratifying as the gift itself.

A Gentleman will open
doors, pull out chairs,
and carry things.
Enigma
Not because she's
helpless or unable,
but because he
wants to show her
that she's valuable
and worthy of respect

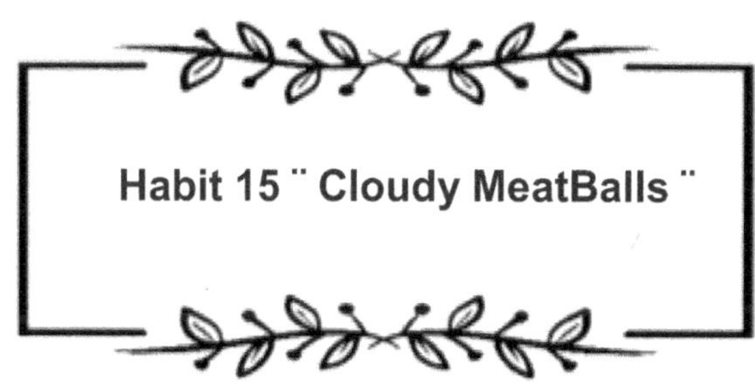

Habit 15 ¨ Cloudy MeatBalls ¨

¨NO¨ is a complete sentence, an explanation is not required. ¨YES¨ is an affirmative response do not interpret it.

Men are gifted with reason and women are gifted with passion. Women are emotion-based and men are logically based. This is a reason why there is always a clash in communications between the couple.

Since women biologically are using the right part of the brain while men are using the left side of the brain there are some issues that can be pacified through recognition of each difference and purpose.

Always remember that when your partner says ¨NO¨ and ¨YES¨ there must be an explanation for it which you need to arrest or assess assertively to avoid confrontation or issues. Women are creative that is why their words are full of colors that you need to find out and the only best way to do it is to ask if she means what she says in a strategic manner to keep away from failing to understand correctly.

When your woman said ¨I love a grand gift on my birthday ¨ then you bought her a fridge or washing machine as a grand and expensive gift then you misunderstood her. As a man, you are detailed oriented than a woman who is big picture-oriented. When she said those words that she loved grand gifts on her birthday perhaps she is referring to not just a material thing but some action grand gesture such as dinner for two, a flower with a cake, and maybe she wanted you both to have another vacation.

A relationship and marital life are not always a bed of roses but it is a battlefield. It is a battle worth saving and each one should win. By learning each other's character through learning her Biological composition which includes her words and her constitution of emotions you will be learning and growing as a couple. Understanding her means comprehending you.

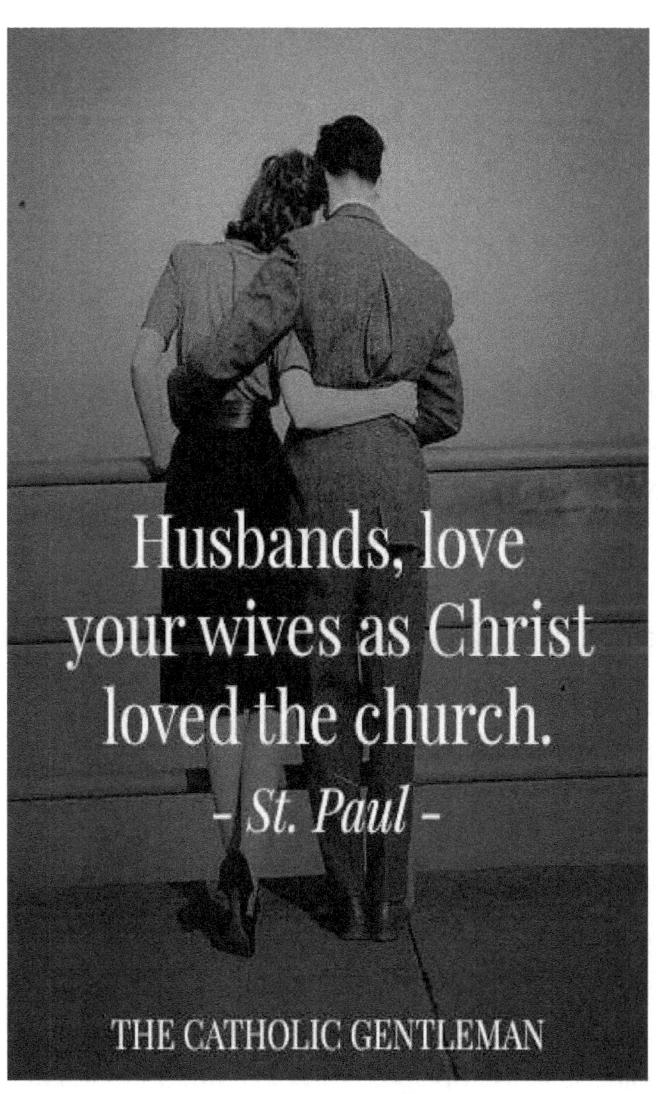
Husbands, love
your wives as Christ
loved the church.
- St. Paul -
THE CATHOLIC GENTLEMAN

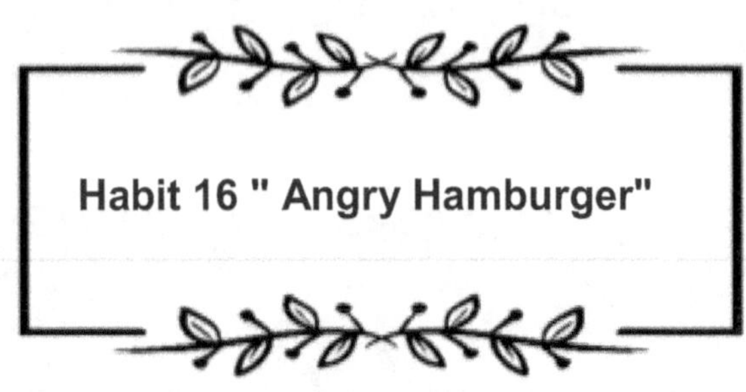

Habit 16 " Angry Hamburger"

How can a woman love a man with a bad temper? A man with a bad temper and who often gets angry with little issues can ruin a relationship. Woman don't want a man who always nags and yell to a certain situation such as displaying boisterous behavior at heavy traffic, having an argument with the food attendant or waiter for giving the wrong drinks, and for initiating an argument each day for some petty issues. It is really toxic and suffocating.

Sometimes we get caught in a situation wherein our mood can be affected by troubles and circumstances that surround us. But the main concern is how you manage and exude a coping mechanism that you remain still in an anger triggering situation. Stillness is different from being apathetic. Stillness is the ability to remain calm and intellectualizing the situation, whereas being apathetic is having a flat affect, being blunt and doing nothing. Realizing the skill to remain calm and rational in a heated discussion or confrontational activity is unparalleled strength. It is the basis of a person's emotional intelligence or in laymen's terms it is called maturity.

Having an easily angered behavior is not helping a relationship but rather it is controlling, hurting, self-destructive, and deprecating. It will just make your woman less trustful and precarious. A happy wife or a happy partner will always find safety and security in your utmost presence. But with your volatile temper, you become a threat and a contributor to her fear and anxiety which on the latter part will be a destruction of your relationship and will further cause more civil and legal disputes.

Anger is not necessarily a bad expression of disbelief or dissatisfaction because in a biblical context Jesus too acts in anger but it is a prime example of righteous anger. When you feel upset or disappointed about the result of a certain situation you may display anger but make sure it is purpose-driven and has a goal of giving a didactic tone of experience.

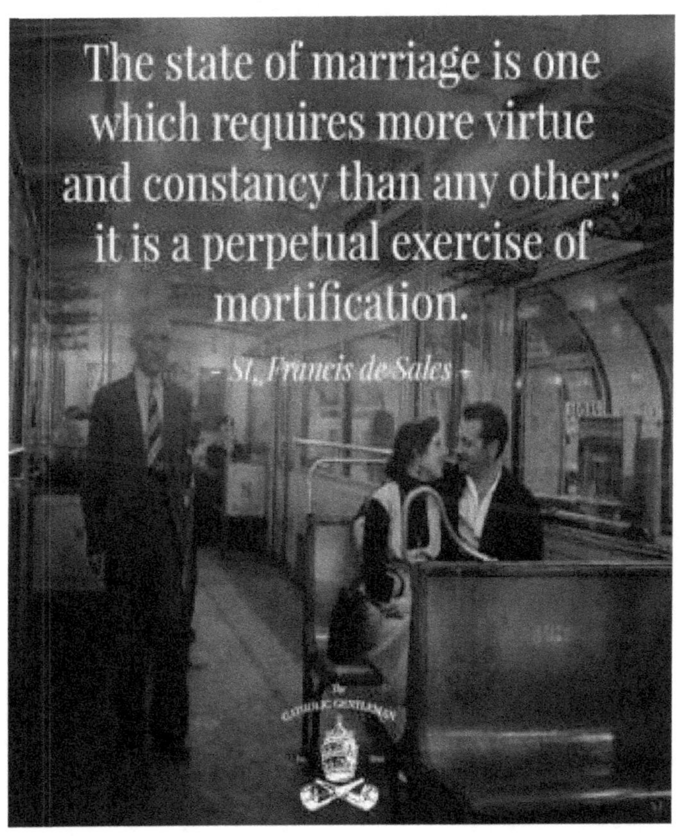
The state of marriage is one which requires more virtue and constancy than any other; it is a perpetual exercise of mortification.
- St. Francis de Sales -

Habit 17 " Be My Ribs, Spareribs"

"So the Lord God caused a deep sleep to fall upon the man, and he slept; then he took one of his ribs and closed up its place with flesh. And the rib that the Lord God had taken from the man he made into a woman and brought her to the man."
—Genesis 2:21–22

From a biblical standpoint, a woman is made from a man's rib which makes a good connection between the two beings. Thus in the manner being exemplified, we can say that man will always be a woman's saving grace, a helper, and a mentor. It is a man's obligation to feed the woman with love, respect, and support all the time.

Your partner will be grateful and experience peace if she finds you comforting her in a moment of grief due to the loss of his parents, she will feel the grace if you stand beside her if she was fired from the job, and surely she will be at ease if you express that you are a co-partner in her gestational period and raising the kids.

A man will always be a confidant and a refuge for a woman who is in distress and in crisis. In a relationship, although you are considered one, you are still an individual with personal issues and needs. Instead of letting your woman find comfort in the presence of her friends why not make use of yourself as a person whom she can trust and deliver all her emotions, uncertainties, and worries? Listening to your wife or partner vent makes you a good and caring partner and even a friend. You don't need to say a word but just listening and giving your time to her is comforting and reassuring. A listening man will serve the intention of removing all the doubts and fears of his better half.

As a man, you must live in a cycle of giving and providing. It is not just about temporal necessities by toiling the earth just to feed your family but above all, it is through giving yourself, sacrificing for the common good of your relationship, and your presence in every squall in the life of your partner and family.

"Now, we must help each other to get to Heaven."
-The Blessed Charles of Austria addressing Empress Zita on 22 October 1911, the day after their wedding.

Habit 18 " Food Give And Forgive

In a relationship or love affair, he who accepts his mistake and asks forgiveness first has control and power. Forgiveness is any relationship guided by love and humility. It is a golden pathway to reconciliation and restoration. Forgiveness is a noble virtue and it should be a practice of a gentleman whether it is asked or must be earned.

Men should always initiate forgiveness as soon as possible when a mistake is committed to keep away from harboring resentment and gathering a pile of hatred in their woman's hearts. You must know that a woman is a creation of emotion and any heartrending pain and afflicting discomfort on her emotion without resolution will have an undesirable effect on her mental health. In marriage or a relationship, a woman will always project onto his immediate family, friends, fellow worker, or men, in general, all the hurts that she experienced from her husband and partner that is why in order to avoid this transition of this ill-feelings, ask for forgiveness is warranted.

A relationship is about compromise. When having trouble and issue with your woman, love will always ask you to step out of your pride and your winning playground. There is power in forgiveness and weakness in withholding it. Being unable to ask forgiveness is a form of slavery. You are a slave of your hatred of pride. And you must break from this chain or it will destroy and tear down the core of goodness and values that is innate in you.

To forgive is a matter of choice and it is deeply rooted in your faith and spirituality. It is a beautiful gift that you can offer to yourself and to your relationship. When it is difficult to forgive it must be the reason that you need to forgive. Life is too short to live in the realm of hatred and ill will. And the ultimate goal of our life is to live in tranquility, free from all atrocities and the burden of unforgiveness.

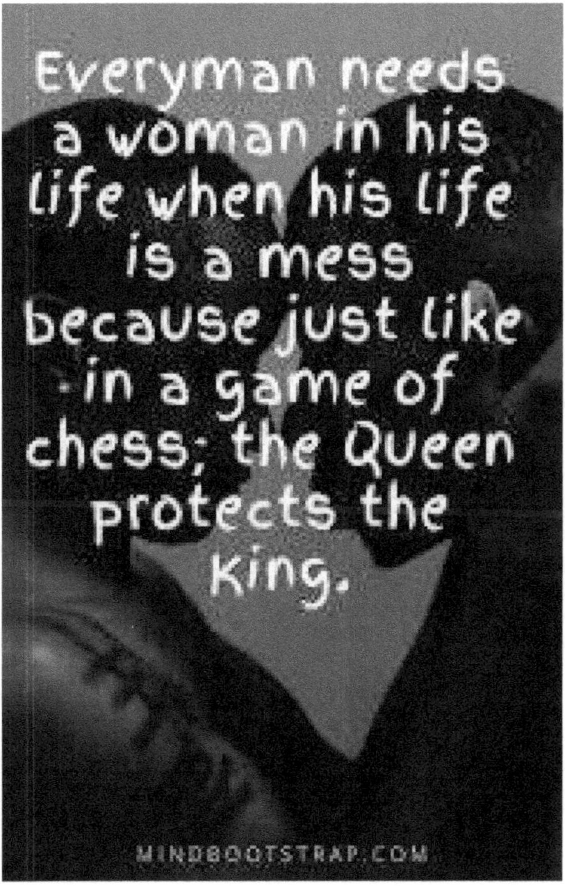

Everyman needs a woman in his life when his life is a mess because just like in a game of chess; the Queen protects the King.

MINDBOOTSTRAP.COM

Habit 19 "Scream, Ice Cream"

Socializing of the couple is an occasion where the lovers can have a fun moment with their friends and acquaintances. It is during social gatherings that a couple is appreciated by their partner as their friends will talk about how appealing and lovely their partner is. It is between the couple's agreement on how much time they can socialize and if they are allowed to drink or not. For there are instances when a couple goes to a party the woman experience annoyance and distress when his husband or boyfriend drinks a lot and causes trouble at the party.

Although your partner is acquainted with or has full knowledge of your smoking, drinking activities, and addiction to mobile games and still accepted you for who you are, however, it should not be a reason for you to continue living in that poor habit. When you are already in a relationship your personal preference and undesirable habit must not overpower and defeat your commitment to your love affair. Your woman's welfare must be put first. Always remember that your action is reflected in your woman's joy and satisfaction. It can only be achieved by your healthy habits and good disposition.

Vices and addiction can jeopardize your relationship by being a deterrent in communication and intimacy. Alcoholic drinking can really affect and interfere with brain communication pathways thus it will also make a difference in your judgment and ways of thinking. Addiction to mobile games, gambling, and partying with your friends can loosen the stitch that binds between you and your woman which will predictably disintegrate the relationship.

A bad habit that is controlling you will control others too specifically your woman. Innate vices such as drinking, alcohol, drugs, and other addiction can be a health problem but with services and help available, it can be effectively dealt with. Your health is also a concern of your partner and if you care and love your partner you must love yourself first by being a source of inspiration through a healthy and amiable lifestyle.

A GREAT MARRIAGE IS NOT WHEN THE 'PERFECT COUPLE' COMES TOGETHER. IT IS WHEN AN IMPERFECT COUPLE LEARNS TO ENJOY THEIR DIFFERENCES.
– DAVE MEURER

Habit 20 “Marinara Sauce Vs. Fettucini Sauce”

"A flower does not think of competing with the flower next to it. It just blooms". -Zen Shin

Although some women like to notice other girls' appearance and style yet it is not equated to comparing herself to that woman but it serves the purpose of being a hero-worship, admiration, and inspiration. If a woman likes to dress up as Scarlet Johansson, it does not follow that she wanted to be compared but rather she is emulating the character and the confidence of the artist.

As a man in a relationship, sometimes you notice similar traits from your partner to a significant person you know. And there would be an occasion that you will find odd how your partner reacts contrastively to a particular instance of the event than someone in your familiarity which will tend you to make a comparison.

The worst thing that you can do with your woman is to compare her with another woman like your mom, your sister, or your ex who is a noun and living a religious life now. It is a bitter pill to swallow for a woman hearing an unsolicited comparison between her and another woman. I bet that you almost hated your father for comparing you to your dog who is more trainable and faithful. Comparing your wife or girlfriend will minimize their capacity to trust and believe in you. It is a toxic aspect of the relationship. When you decided to have this woman as your partner and wife you are not choosing her because of her appearance, talents, and social status in the community but you selected her because you believe that her soul, love, and strength are suited to your spirit for a lifetime commitment.

Sometimes comparison of your woman can happen with your observation of social media. There are instances that you feel envy about how a certain couple shows their affection on every web network platform. Take into consideration that a happy couple will never publish and announce their happiness on a public network. A happy couple is someone who embraces love and togetherness in an atmosphere that both of you believe in without the validation of others.

When you see each other in the morning and again at night, practice pausing to think before you speak to your spouse and kids.

Make every effort to give words of life and win together in your marriage and family!

LiveYourBestMarriage.com

Habit 21 "Overjoy ChickenJoy"

The most challenging part of being a man in a relationship is knowing what matters and deciding what is productive and fruitful. A successful relationship is not about grandeur, happiness, and vanity but it is about acceptance, satisfaction, and fulfillment of joy.

Happiness is not parallel to joy and a woman's happiness will never be a woman's joy. It is not identical, both have a distinct magnitude. Happiness is a complex feeling that comes over when something pleasant and good happens. It is dependent on external happenings. Joy is evoked by peace and transcendence experience beyond the normal and physical level. Women wanted to have joy deep inside their hearts and soul. And a man should assess if he is bequeathing happiness or joy to his partner.

Giving gifts and other surprises will give happiness but understanding and care provide joy. If you are seeking happiness in a relationship, you will keep hoping that everything is enough. When your purpose as a man to your woman is to provide something that will make her happy, you will later have a series of "what if" lists. But if you pursue joy in your affair you will discover existential longevity in your relationship with an authentic certainty that through rough and smooth you will still end up as a lover for life.

Happiness is a process of life, for instance, you will be happy because she made you a cup of coffee and disappointed when she didn't. Joy is a way of life wherein you give your partner an assurance that your unwavering love will linger through everything. When a man has a joyful spirit his relationship will foster truth, respect, and peace.

Joy is closely linked to spirituality. When a man discovers his faith and evaluates his life, he will find joy. That joy will bring goodness to his relationship. And a joyful man can transform his woman into a marvelous grace who encompasses love and cheerfulness.

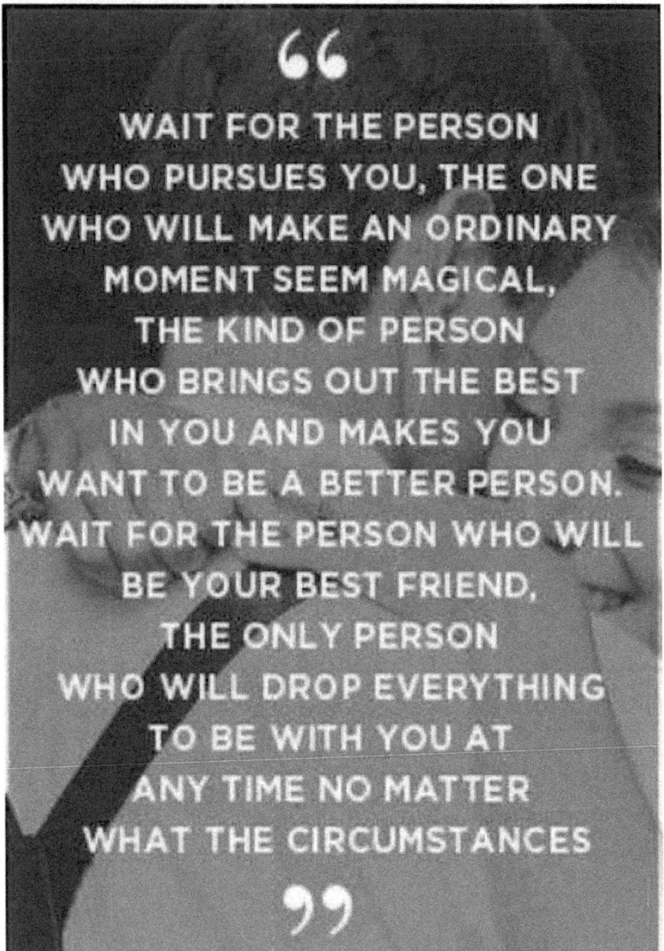

“

WAIT FOR THE PERSON
WHO PURSUES YOU, THE ONE
WHO WILL MAKE AN ORDINARY
MOMENT SEEM MAGICAL,
THE KIND OF PERSON
WHO BRINGS OUT THE BEST
IN YOU AND MAKES YOU
WANT TO BE A BETTER PERSON.
WAIT FOR THE PERSON WHO WILL
BE YOUR BEST FRIEND,
THE ONLY PERSON
WHO WILL DROP EVERYTHING
TO BE WITH YOU AT
ANY TIME NO MATTER
WHAT THE CIRCUMSTANCES

”

All men are created for greatness. He should serve as a beacon of hope, transforming lives and inculcating love in everyone most importantly to his family, his relationship, partner, wife, and children.

The task of being an inspiring gentleman is a big shoe to fill but with constant and persistent exercise you will master the art of each habit.

Men are wonderfully made for an important purpose. Civilization was made because of men's continuance and tenacity. Along with this are women who perform support for the betterment of society. If every man rediscovers his great significance and value, there will be a dramatic change in our society which will transcend how to treat every woman with dignity, love, respect, and equity.

ABOUT THE AUTHORS

Ana Rita Reyes is an educator, ECE Program Director, Admin, and Co-Creator of FIL-AM SOUTH BAY COMMUNITY, Commissioner of Library and Education in District 5 San Jose, California, Motivational Speaker, Transformational Life Coach, and a Catechist.

She is been the author of 3 books. Her autobiography "Woman Of Hope" and self-help books "365 Days" and "I am Worthy" co-authored 2 self-help guide books for a couple "Understanding Him" and "Understanding Her".

She is also a writer and co-author of 3 Children's book which showcases Philippine Culture, and Stories about values and teachers.

She is featured on the cover of Planet Magazines where her stories and works were depicted.

She has been featured on TV for her altruistic work in the community, interviewed on Radio and podcasts, and received various awards and recognition for her unparalleled service to the community. Interviewed with local, national, and international media outlets like Canada, the USA, and the Philippines.

Internationally earned a Doctorate in Literature through her 1st book Woman of Hope.

Her life is dedicated to being a service to the community through service, altruism, and promoting physical, emotional, intellectual, and spiritual change through her blogs and writings on social media and daily Facebook Live inspirational talk and guest speaker for school.

She has a little foundation with a friend called "Woman Of Hope Foundation" by the annual Christmas "Adopt A Kid" and they are supporting selected kids in their schooling.

Her passion and dedication to her career and personal endeavors are driven by love and selflessness for the greater glory of God.

Bimby Macbs is a Registered Nurse in the Philippines and has worked in Academe and Pharmaceutical Companies.

He decides to discontinue his job and focus on freelance writing, catechism, and in evangelization.

He has training in the human temperament, love languages, and psycho-spiritual integration.

He is a career coach (helping students in matching their character to their career toward a successful college program and professional life) lyricist, poet, writer, event host, organizer, administrator of local celebrities' online platform, and author of a published children's book.

"When You Really Love Someone"
~Alicia Keys

I'm a woman
Lord knows it's hard
I need a real man
To give me what I need
Sweet attention
Love and tenderness
When it's real, it's unconditional
I'm telling y'all

'Cause a man just ain't a man if he ain't man enough
To love you when you're right
Love you when you're wrong
Love you when you're weak
Love you when you're strong
Take you higher
When the world's got you feeling low
He's giving you his last
'Cause he's thinking of you first
Giving comfort when he's thinking that you're hurt
That's what done when you really love someone
I'm telling y'all, I'm telling y'all

'Cause you're a real man
And lord knows it's hard
Sometimes you just need a woman's touch
Sweet affection
Love and support
When it's real, it's unconditional
I'm telling y'all

Oh, 'cause a woman ain't a woman if she ain't
woman enough
To love you when you're right
Love you when You're wrong
Love you when you're weak
Love you when you're strong
Take you higher, oh
When the world's got you feeling low
She giving you her best
Even when you're at your worst
Giving 'comfort when' she's thinking that you're hurt
That's what's done when you really love someone
I'm telling y'all, I'm telling y'all

Sometimes you wanna argue, sometimes you wanna fight
Sometimes it's gonna feel like it'll never be right
But something so strong keeps you holding on
It's don't make sense, but it makes a good song

'Cause a man just ain't a man if he ain't man enough
To love you when you're right
Love you when you're wrong
Love you when you're weak
Love you when you're strong
Take you higher
When the world's got you feeling low
He's giving you his last
'Cause he's thinking of you first
Giving comfort when he's thinking that you're hurt
That's what's done when you really love someone
I'm telling y'all, I'm telling y'all

I'm telling y'all that a woman ain't a woman
If she ain't woman enough
To love you when you're right
Love you when you're wrong
Love you when you're weak
Love you when you're strong
Take you higher (And higher)
When the world's got you feeling low
She giving you her best
Even when you're at your worst
Giving comfort when she's thinking that you're hurt
That's what's done when you really love someone
I'm telling y'all, I'm telling y'all

www.ingramcontent.com/pod-product-compliance
Lightning Source LLC
LaVergne TN
LVHW010453160826
845677LV00012B/2473

* 9 7 8 6 2 1 4 7 0 4 6 3 7 *